# Karmic Astrology

## Mastering Key Life Lessons for All 12 Zodiac Signs

### Copper Moon

# Contents

# DISCLAIMER (READ THIS FIRST!)

Thank you for exploring the world of Karmic Astrology with me. Please be fully aware, now, that this book exists solely as a tool or assistant designed to help us continue advancing along our soul's evolutionary journeys. As a result, please understand that this is not a book built around compliments and flattering remarks about your zodiac sign. You already know how quick-witted Geminis can be; the selfless giving Virgos exhibit; the magnetic persona that is Leo; the enchanting mysteries teased by Pisces; and so on.

**I REPEAT:** THIS BOOK IS NOT HERE TO BE YOUR HYPE MAN, BUTTER YOUR BREAD, OR GROW YOUR HEAD.

This book exists for one reason, and one reason alone: to help us continue advancing along our soul's evolutionary journeys. Therefore, it will focus less on each sign's common positives, and instead highlight the negatives. Please don't be offended, slighted, or discouraged. There's a big difference between constructive criticism, and false judgments. This material relates to the former, and not the latter.

By understanding our potential drawbacks and transmuting them – in much the same way as the alchemist was known for turning lead to gold – we will add even more strengths to our personal armory. This will assist not only us individually, but also collectively, as we continue to battle spiritually – caught between forces and natures of lower and higher frequencies – for the sake of fully awakening to true self.

Finally: we live in a very busy world now. Everyone's time is precious. As this book is focused directly on karma as it relates to each sun sign, it has been kept as straightforward and to the point as possible. No fluff, and no added padding. Whether you know a little, or a lot, about astrology. I've read many books in my time that used over 300 pages to convey what could have easily been stated more simply in less than one hundred. So, let me not arrest more of your precious time than is needed to relay the message.

May this simple little book, in its own measure, help you on your personal path to that divine self.

(C. Moon)

———

Note: If, after completing this book, you still have questions concerning any of the concepts or content presented here – or if you would like to receive a free general birth chart reading from the author – you can reach out directly using the publisher's email here: info@aliopublishing.com

# Introduction: Before We Begin...

I have a question for you. Can you think of at least one subject that has consistently gripped people's attention, and sparked their curiosity, for thousands of years and across continents? (Excluding basic essentials such as food and procreating) Well, I can. Few topics of interest can claim the accolades of attention astrology has both attained and maintained.

As one of civilization's oldest surviving sciences and hobbies, it has been a perennial source of both knowledge and entertainment for individuals that effortlessly transcends cultures. Even those who call it bogus still tend to know and claim their sun sign! (Even if they don't realize it's the sun sign, specifically – and that we have a moon, ascendant, and many more placements as well that constitute our character.) While the average admirer will typically never approach the deep mathematical rabbit holes in which the subject can dive – preferring to interact with its elements on an informal surface level – they are no less captivated and enthralled by the psychological and physiological self-portraits painted by astrology.

From tropical and Chinese, to Arabic and Vedic (sidereal), there are a variety of distinct disciplines and interpretation methods of this science of the stars, as well; similar, in a sense, to how a single religion can contain many branches or denominations. Due to the vast array of interpretation methods at hand – as well as the tendency of time to water down the origins and purpose of things – astrology is frequently discounted, discredited, and even denounced.

Most go with arguments along the lines of likening it to a "pseudo-science", or against God (a typical Christian stance). Both accusations are ironic, given how rigorously-precise and scientific astrological calculations are, and the intimidating number of references made in the King James Bible to astrology (one example being the 12 gates of Jerusalem); however much they may "hide" in plain sight.

Not too far from the study of the stars, is the concept and belief in karma. Another often misunderstood term outside of its religious context, karma can be simply summed up as the children of one's choices. In other words: "you will reap what you have sown." Many who have learned of karma outside of its culture of origin tend to think of it in terms of something bad or undesirable happening in someone's life... but that is simply not the universal intent. (And speaking of which: please don't be one of those out there wishing "bad karma" on someone whom you feel has wronged you in some way, as doing so is far more likely to deliver that unwanted wish to your front doorstep instead.)

Karma is impartial. Neither good nor bad, it only returns to you what you have given. And whether what we receive be labeled pleasant or painful, it all serves a higher purpose: love, spiritual growth, and self-realization. In that sense, we can think of karma as our "homeroom teacher". No matter where you travel to throughout the school grounds as you switch classes, at some point, you will find yourself back in your homeroom once more.

What's fascinating is the interplay between astrology and karma. Based on the exact coordinates of one's birth, a natal chart can be mapped revealing many under-the-surface aspects of the personality... in addition to clues concerning karma cleared, and karma closing in. Again, it's nothing to be feared. In fact, embrace it! In particular, the north node and south node of the birth chart can reveal significant details behind the nature of one's own life lessons. This includes, how to pass them.

That being said, it is not necessary for everyone to know their exact time and place of birth to have a natal chart constructed, just to identify what lessons are the most pressing in their current lifetime.(*) Maybe you don't have a birth certificate. Perhaps nobody in your family kept birth records. In any case, most of us at least know the month and day we were born; and believe it or not, that is all the data that will be needed here.

As much as it would be worthwhile to explore those deeper elements... that is not the purpose of this book. To do so would lead us away on a distraction from its primary intention, which is simply this: to identify the most common life lessons for each of the 12 sun signs – and how to pass their tests. If there's a desire or a demand expressed in the future from enough readers, I'd be thrilled to offer a follow-up that goes all in with the elements and inner workings of the birth chart. For now however, simply focusing on the sun sign – as the sun represents our soul – is more than sufficient to supply us with ample nourishment for the soul's sustenance.

Also, we will be looking at things strictly from a Western or Tropical perspective here, as most of my readers will likely be more familiar with that branch of the star sciences. Personally, I make use of both Western and Eastern (specifically, Vedic) methods, and recommend both for different reasons. As a wise associate of mine once said: "Sidereal astrology is scientific; Tropical astrology is magical." Without a doubt, sidereal is simply more mathematically accurate, as its days are not based on the procession of the static and ever-problematic Gregorian calendar. (Side note: for those interested in Vedic or sidereal astrology, a book introducing it to beginners is in the works.)

Despite this, there is a certain intangible, even magical quality to Western astrology that causes it to resonate with millions, if not billions of individuals. Even if on paper it shouldn't be true; by most accounts, it appears to be on the nose more often than not. So even if one were of the opinion that astrology, as well as other related areas of esoterics, were nothing more than recorded history's most enduring mass placebo effect (and this is coming from someone who for over a decade denied astrology's merits and validity as a fluke of false beliefs), even that would not counteract or cancel its presence.

It might not be "real" in the same sense that a redwood or raven is. However, it is certainly just as "real" as next Tuesday, or someone's love for you. Think about it: would Tuesdays ever exist, if mankind hadn't committed to considering them conceptually? There are many things in this life that can't be touched with fingers or toes, and only persist in existence by our honest believing in them.

All is mind – including time, and stars, and space. And with that having been said: let us begin the exploration of our collective karmic journey – courtesy of the 12 tropical sun signs!

———

(*) – Even if a birth chart is not required in order for you to master your life

lessons and attain greater self-realization...
it certainly doesn't hurt in that area! I have
revisited my own chart again & again for
decades now, and it has never failed to shed
light on a new angle. If you're curious to
learn more beyond your sun or moon sign,
there are several reliable online resources
to map and analyze your personal birth
chart. These urls will be listed at the back of
this book.

# 1

# ARIES: The Pioneer

**Affirmation:** "I am capable of anything I decide to do."

Of all the zodiac signs, Aries is the one that is least likely to be hiding out in the background, or the hardest to detect, or the most reserved. More often that not, they are loved – or loathed – by those around them, with a hot intensity that matches their own energetic fingerprint.

Not every Aries may be a leader or pioneer in the strictest sense of those words... but they all have the potential inside them to be. Typically, these are the folks around us who inspire through direct action, wear their heart on their sleeves, chase the nearest rainbows, and speak their mind when something doesn't seem right.

## Common Karmic Lessons

With so much power and passion etched in their makeup, what could an Aries possibly have to learn in this lifetime? A lot. That's not a knock against them, by the way – just confirmation that they are as human as their zodiac brothers and sisters. As the first sign in tropical astrology, they are also the ruler of the first house governing physical appearance, and ruled by Mars.

They are nothing if not a finely-woven blanket of firsts. The first zodiac sign. The first fire sign. The first cardinal sign. The first sign of Spring. The first masculine sign. See a pattern? Yes; rare is the Aries that doesn't love to be first. If the affirmation "I AM" had to be assigned to one specific zodiac sign, then it would no doubt be the ram. Sometimes, this manifests as an unflattering tendency of an Aries to always see themselves as right, regardless of the situation.

Despite not being an earth or a fixed sign, they can also be shockingly stubborn and set in certain ways as well, especially as it pertains to personal habits and behaviors. Aries often think very highly of themselves. This may be due to an intuitive awareness of their inner strength. Ironically, this sometimes leads to false projections of anxiety and insecurity, particularly if the Aries in question is living an external reality that clashes or contradicts the one within them.

It isn't uncommon, unfortunately, for Aries with challenging childhoods to develop a tendency to thwart their own powerful imagination, act unnaturally timid, and hold back their desires or thoughts for the sake of not rocking boats. The evolved Aries will be capable of showing compassion and consideration for others, without having to stifle their own voice in the process.

## Karmic Clues by Nodes

Opposite to Aries is the seventh house ruler, Libra. In everyone's birth chart there is a North Node (also known as Rahu), and a South Node (also known as Ketu). The sign our South Node is in speaks to where we're coming from as a sentient soul – or in other words, our recent past lives, and predominant mindsets and skillsets as a result. The sign of our North Node – which is always approximate 180 degrees apart from the South Node, just as Libra always rests 180 degrees from Aries – represents the areas of life we are less comfortable in or accustomed to, but will lead to the most growth and fulfillment for the soul, when pursued and developed.

In other words, the South Node sign can be said to reflect the things that come easy to us (our comfort zones), whereas the North Node represents the things that only come with conscious, deliberate effort (our greatest growth opportunities). Understanding the Nodes and their role in our destiny (that is, destination), is vital to understanding our karmic astrology. For

Aries, understanding the Libra archetype is just as beneficial as understanding their own Aries nature.

If you know you have Aries as your South Node, you probably will gain even more benefits by reading the Libra chapter as well. Pay special attention to the dynamics of your relationships with others. (This goes for friends, family, business, and intimate.) Making great strides to promote fairness and justice in all exchanges will highly benefit you and your reputation.

## Root Karmic Triggers for Aries

The phrase "root karmic triggers" refers to people, things, and situations that are most likely to reflect or highlight a person's karma from birth, based on their sun sign. Think of them as "sensitive" areas, if you like. These often contain deep vulnerabilities within the psyche of the Aries archetype, and hide an uncultivated wellspring of great, transcendent power if the appropriate conscious work is put in to transform weakness into strength.

It is highly generalized – no two Aries are exactly the same, after all – and should be taken with a reasonable grain of salt. However, even with the potential for some margin of error, these triggers may prove to be a common theme for many who identify under the sign of Aries; even those who may not have their natal sun in Aries (such as a moon in Aries, Aries rising, or Mars in Aries; as examples). As a result, it is highly recommended that every Aries individual examine these areas in their life, and utilize them as opportunities to evolve:

## THE FOREHEAD REGION

Its not a coincidence that many Aries-dominant people have suffered from headaches, migraines, and allergic reactions. It is suggested that they make sure to spend plenty of time outdoors in nature, and make sure to avoid dehydration. Physical health may suffer if inspired ideas are ignored, or pushed aside, for prolonged periods of time.

Most Aries will fare better in the long run working careers that favor physical movement over excessive periods of sitting, keeping them out of their head, and less susceptible to nerve issues.

## EARLY CHILDHOOD

While its an obvious truth that every person is greatly affected by their earliest years, with an Aries this is especially the case. If their naturally-exuberant curiosity, playfulness and physicality are met with rigidity or chastisement, it could result in the young ram clamming up, and cutting parts of themselves off psychologically.

This arrested development could have serious ramifications in their adult life if not checked or resolved.

## SELF IDENTITY

In a cultural climate where people identify with objects, creeds, and even genders that did not exist less than one century prior, it has never been more challenging to be an Aries. This is especially true for the vocal Aries living in an era where political correctness has made it too easy to ostracize and stigmatize people based on something they said.

Even so, it will not profit any Aries in the long run to make it a habit of bottling up their thoughts. In fact, it will only lead to fractures in their relationships with others, most likely. Also: Aries can be secretly self-conscious of their body image. They should do their best to feel good in their skin, and develop a certain degree of indifference towards the unsolicited opinions of others.

## In Short...

The most pressing lesson for sun Aries – as well as individuals with prominent Aries birth chart placements – is two-fold. It is having the courage to stand tall in one's truth and be a leader, even when there appears to be nobody following you. (This is one of those lies we tend to tell ourselves; I assure you that every strong Aries has someone in their environment who is watching them intently to some degree, whether or not the ram in question is aware of this.)

Simultaneously, this requires a willingness to work with others, and consider what's best for not only them individually, but also their group, community, or society. Be a leader who is able to trust others enough to depend on them as well. In any event, courage is the keyword here. Contrary to popular belief, not every person born in March or April is a willing trailblazer that's ready at a moment's notice to set other's expectations on fire while challenging all opposers.

Often in life, our greatest strengths require the most patience and preparation in order to reach full maturation. If we were to select from the generous plethora of talented Aries vocalists that the past century has

blessed the world with, as an example
– from Marvin Gaye to Mariah Carey –
you would have a daunting task on your
hands, if you were determined to find
one that had displayed such breathtaking
skills without practice and repetition. Talent
can take someone a long way; this is
true, to an extent. Discipline, repetition,
and perseverance will take anyone much
farther though – regardless of how much
"talent" they started out with.

I state all that to say this: being born
an Aries doesn't automatically make
someone courageous, no more than being
born a Cancer protective of loved ones,
a Libra outgoing and talkative, or a
Capricorn motivated to succeed. Having
an innate quality or qualities in us isn't
sufficient to ensure they manifest in our
three-dimensional experience. All it takes

is a significant number of unpleasing or traumatic life experiences – perhaps coupled with aspects in the natal birth chart working to undermine what might otherwise be given tendencies – and **BLAM!** Just like that: one can fall astray.

If you identify with Aries, ask yourself the following questions:

1. What am I most afraid of doing in life?

2. How am I confronting this fear, if at all?

3. When was the last time I asked someone for help with this?

Answer these questions honestly, and reflect on each of them afterwards to ascertain where you currently are on your life journey karmically.

# TAURUS: NURTURE OUT; NURTURE IN

**Affirmation:** "I am more than what I provide for others."

Like Ferdinand the Bull, a Taurus is, at heart, a patron of peace. Typically regarded as being among some of the most patient people among us, it truly takes a lot to push a well-balanced bull to swap relaxation with rage. (And trust me: you don't want to be the one doing the pushing.) Most Taureans naturally exude a calm and dignified demeanor that wins others over without effort.

Despite this, many Taurus sun signs struggle with self-worth internally, lacking the same great confidence many assume them to possess. To truly understand the inner workings of a Taurus, one must know what that Taurus most associates with their values in life; whether it be a material thing, or a spiritual belief.

## Common Karmic Lessons

How is it that even despite having strings of loved ones and admirers, so many Taureans can hold such a low opinion of themselves? It may be in part an unfortunate by-product of their natural inclination to build and produce; although these are obviously not negative traits. As the second sign in tropical astrology,

Taurus is the ruler of the second house governing assets and material possessions, and is ruled by Venus. Sometimes, there is a tendency here to project their values on others, which can lead to the belief that in order to be loved or receive love, they must have something to show for it.

Unlike Aries, Taurus is a fixed, feminine sign. They are more down-to-earth and practical than most other signs, and are known quite well to be very hard workers. As they are willing to go to great lengths to attain the finer things in life (whatever they may define those as), it can lead to feelings such as impostor syndrome, of not being good enough, or of never quite having enough. The less spiritually-grounded and the more materially-minded the Taurus is, the more pronounced the problem tends to manifest.

Some examples of this are shown in the model or actress who has every surgery known to modern man performed on her body in order to look as "youthful" as possible; the athlete who abuses steroids to maintain peak performance; the shrewd hustler or businessman who decides to "fake it 'til they make it". Oftentimes, there can be an imbalance between what the self truly desires to give, versus what the individual in question thinks they need to give to appease others. Overworking is a common result here.

Ultimately, it is up to each Taurus to separate what they own, and what they do, from what they are worth, which is immeasurable by comparison. The evolved Taurus will recognize their own value independent of physical possessions, outside opinions, or external conditions.

## Karmic Clues by Nodes

Opposite to Taurus is the eighth house ruler, Scorpio. In everyone's birth chart there is a North Node (also known as Rahu), and a South Node (also known as Ketu). The sign our South Node is in speaks to where we're coming from as a sentient soul – or in other words, our recent past lives, and predominant mindsets and skillsets as a result. The sign of our North Node – which is always approximate 180 degrees apart from the South Node, just as Scorpio always rests 180 degrees opposite Taurus – represents the areas of life we are less comfortable in or accustomed to, but will lead to the most growth and fulfillment for the soul, when pursued and developed.

In other words, the South Node sign can be said to reflect the things that come easy to us (our comfort zones), whereas the North Node represents the things that only come with conscious, deliberate effort (our greatest growth opportunities). Understanding the Nodes and their role in our destiny (that is, destination), is vital to understanding our karmic astrology. For Taurus, understanding the Scorpio archetype is just as beneficial as understanding their own Taurus nature.

If you know you have Taurus as your South Node, you probably will gain even more benefits by reading the Scorpio chapter as well. Also: pay special attention to your long-term life and career goals, nurture your close personal relationships, and cultivate a healthy sex life (if its of interest to you).

## Root Karmic Triggers for Taurus

The phrase "root karmic triggers" refers to people, things, and situations that are most likely to reflect or highlight a person's karma from birth, based on their sun sign. Think of them as "sensitive" areas, if you like. These often contain deep vulnerabilities within the psyche of the Taurus archetype, and hide an uncultivated wellspring of great, transcendent power if the appropriate conscious work is put in to transform weakness into strength.

It is highly generalized – no two Taureans are exactly the same, after all – and should be taken with a reasonable grain of salt. However, even with the potential for some margin of error, these triggers may prove to be a common theme for many who identify under the sign of Taurus; even those who may not have their natal sun in Taurus (such as a Mars or moon in

Taurus, as examples). As a result, it is highly recommended that every Taurus individual examine these areas in their life, and utilize them as opportunities to evolve:

## THE THROAT REGION

Its not uncommon for a Taurus to have a pleasant speaking voice, and many make great singers. This can become a hidden talent, however, in those individuals that neglect cultivating their Venusian gifts. Where low self-esteem is prevalent, their confidence in public speaking may be at risk. Thyroid complications are a potential threat as well, but can be prevented with right thinking, as well as right eating.

## THE NEED TO THINGS

While there are certainly those exceptions to the rule, it is not unusual for a Taurus man or woman to demonstrate a taste for life's "finer things". Whether we're talking 5-star cuisine, or brand name attire, the typical Taurus places a lot of weight on physical appearances. By the same token, they tend to quietly delight in surrounding themselves with their choice creature comforts. One example of this is manifested in the avid coin collector; or, the diehard action figure fan who has an entire room of their home dedicated to displaying their plastic trophies for visitors to bask in.

As a Taurus, do take care not to place too much importance on what you own, or over-inflate how others perceive you from a conditional, transactionary standpoint.

## A "BORING" COMPLEX

Oddly enough... quite a few Taureans harbor a deep-rooted belief that they are... boring. (Don't ask me.) I don't know where this stems from, but I've known several bulls who echoed this false self-sentiment.

If anything, it may be an indication that the individual is holding something in them back, and again, portraying a version of themselves to the world that they find more acceptable, rather than the authentic them. As Taurus is the opposite sign of Scorpio, its likely that some of that sign's highly self-critical aspects take shape in Taurus' shadow side. (Shadow meaning one's unknown, hidden or suppressed aspects; not "bad" or evil. Light and shadow are two sides of the same coin, after all.)

## In Short...

The most pressing lesson for sun Taurus – as well as individuals with prominent Taurus birth chart placements – is to recognize their inherent abundance

and worth. To know that their value
is not directly tied to, or dependent
upon anything they possess or produce
externally, is vital to the individual leading
a self-fulfilling existence.

Of course, it doesn't help that in many parts
of the world we currently live in a very
carnal, surface-driven, materialistic society.
With so much stress and fears centered
around daily survival, finding a partner,
providing, and making ends meet, one can't
fault a Taurus completely for leaning into
a provider's mentality. Also, it's a perfectly
acceptable trait to have.

Just please: don't make the mistake of
thinking that's all you are to the world!

If you identify with Taurus, ask yourself the
following questions:

    1. What do I value most in life?

2. What – or who – am I most afraid of losing?

3. What is my primary motivation in choosing my career of choice?

Answer these questions honestly, and reflect on each of them afterwards to ascertain where you currently are on your life journey from a karma-clearing perspective.

# GEMINI: LIKE A BLOWING BREEZE

**Affirmation:** "I am the cushion that softens life's toughest blows."

Flirty, witty, and a head-space that never has a vacancy: these a few ways to describe your average Gemini. Their naturally precocious and sprite-like nature can at times cause them to be one of the most misunderstood signs of the zodiac. Often labeled as "two-faced" or "wishy-washy", some folks have harbored a harsh view of the sign associated with the twins. In truth, mercurial Geminis are meant to liven up the scene with their high spirits and colorful banter, operating best when maintaining a "glass half-filled" mentality.

First, we ought to ask ourselves what makes the Gemini tick. Before now, we were examining a ram, and a bull. With Gemini – the first air sign, and mutable sign – we have our first man-based archetype. As this would imply, Geminis tend to be very cerebral, and extensive thinkers. This is fair, as they are ruled by Mercury. Of course, this ability of theirs will fail to flourish into its full potential if they fall into the temptation of incessant thoughts and over-thinking that lead to so many mixed feelings and sleepless nights.

## Common Karmic Lessons

As a mutable sign, Geminis can be very fickle, flighty, and flirty. And not just in regards to personal relationships, but also in work, business, and any social areas. On the flip-side, a Gemini is quite capable of displaying obsessive tendencies when they become mentally fixated on a particular person or thing – to the extent that virtually all else ceases to exist, in their mind. Such Geminis must learn to cultivate a sense of inner balance by not just living life inside of their head, but outside as well.

Also, some Geminis may get carried away with a certain idea or philosophy or opinion of the moment, without doing the research to back it up. They're usually great at spinning words together on the fly, which is enough to fool the average listener. But, if they attempt to posture in front of someone more knowledgeable in that given area, they may end up making themselves look bad.

All Geminis require mental stimulation, but they should make sure to balance this out with adequate physical exertion as well, to prevent possible mental disorders down the road. They can prove to be a viable intellectual asset to any group or team, and should avoid becoming too closed off from the world by staying involved in their families, friend groups, and extra-curricular organizations.

As much as Geminis love picking up and sharing information, it is important that they recognize that not all information is knowledge. In order to avoid dimming their natural youthful glow, and becoming over-burdened by mental conflicts, it is highly recommended that they take the occasional data detox. This includes turning off the phone, days off from social media, and being very discerning concerning what types of media are consumed. By preserving their lightheartedness, they can uplift others by simply being present.

## Karmic Clues by Nodes

Opposite to Gemini is the ninth house ruler, Sagittarius. In everyone's birth chart there is a North Node (also known as Rahu), and a South Node (also known as Ketu). The sign our South Node is in speaks to where we're coming from as a sentient soul – or in other words, our recent past lives, and predominant mindsets and skillsets as a result. The sign of our North Node – which is always approximate 180 degrees apart from the South Node, just as Sagittarius always rests 180 degrees opposite Gemini

– represents the areas of life we are less comfortable in or accustomed to, but will lead to the most growth and fulfillment for the soul, when pursued and developed.

In other words, the South Node sign can be said to reflect the things that come easy to us (our comfort zones), whereas the North Node represents the things that only come with conscious, deliberate effort (our greatest growth opportunities). Understanding the Nodes and their role in our destiny (that is, destination), is vital to understanding our karmic astrology. For Gemini, understanding the Sagittarius archetype is just as beneficial as understanding their own dual nature.

If you know you have Gemini as your South Node, you probably will gain even more benefits by reading the Sagittarius chapter as well. Pay close attention to the impact your cultural, religious, and educational backgrounds have on your life. And travel as often as you can!

## Root Karmic Triggers for Gemini

The phrase "root karmic triggers" refers to people, things, and situations that are most likely to reflect or highlight a person's karma from birth, based on their sun sign. Think of them as "sensitive" areas, if you like. These often contain deep vulnerabilities within the psyche of the Gemini archetype, and hide an uncultivated wellspring of great, transcendent power if the appropriate conscious work is put in to transform weakness into strength.

It is highly generalized – no two Geminis are exactly the same, after all – and should be taken with a reasonable grain of salt.

However, even with the potential for some margin of error, these triggers may prove to be a common theme for many who identify under the sign of Gemini; even those who may not have their natal sun in Gemini (such as a Gemini rising, for example). As a result, it is highly recommended that every Gemini individual examine these areas in their life, and utilize them as opportunities to evolve:

## THE COMMUNITY

Geminis generally thrive in social settings of all sizes. This can, of course, be impacted by early childhood experiences. A happy Gemini, is a Gemini who feels like an active, contributing member of their community.

This could be at the workplace, in the home, or any other organized group. Its not uncommon for Geminis to be involved with local affairs as well, such as a neighborhood committee. If you are a Gemini and you feel something is missing in life, get better acquainted with the area you live, and look for ways you can get involved firsthand.

## SIBLINGS

Growing up with (or without) siblings can have a tremendous influence on a Gemini's development. Whether a brother or sister, Geminis tend to view their siblings as one of their most important relationships; all things being healthy and equal. That having been said, if you do have any brothers or sisters, if you experienced any trauma or hardships in these relationships, take some time to deeply reflect on how you were affected.

## FLIGHTS OF FANCY

A problem that can plague all the air signs, Gemini is not immune to occasionally drifting off from reality. I'm sure your head is a fine place to visit... but do you really want to live there 24/7? Make time for the outdoors, get plenty of fresh air, and find ways to ground in the natural world. Cultivate silence and peace, so that your mind may remain as fresh and lively as the day it debuted.

**In Short...**

The most pressing lesson for sun Gemini – as well as individuals with prominent Gemini birth chart placements – is learning how to express themselves effectively without compromising their pure spirit.

Avoid living exclusively in your head, or holding to passing views and opinions that haven't been anchored or put to the fire. This is not to say all Geminis display a tendency to relay mostly surface-level knowledge, or that they aren't capable of profound, truly thought-provoking insights. They are. But these are qualities that don't always come naturally (especially in a cultural climate of cheap thrills and instant gratification) and more often than not, must be cultivated over time.

In their power, Geminis are capable of spreading much fun and positivity. They relish making others laugh, and turning frowns upside down. To be this ray of light – without the superficiality, and perhaps a bit of elven mischievousness – is a noble aim for the sign of the twins.

If you identify with Gemini, ask yourself the following questions:

1. What do I express to others when I

communicate?

2. In what ways am I contributing creatively?

3. How am I preserving and nurturing my inner child?

Answer each question honestly, and reflect on them afterwards to determine how you are currently progressing on your karmic journey.

# 4

# CANCER: THE GUARDED GUARDIAN

**Affirmation:** "I am the physical manifestation of the divine nurturer, being naturally abundant."

As the Summer Solstice unfolds in the Western World, the zodiac transitions into the second cardinal sign of Cancer. Like Aries, Cancers are born trailblazers and innovators; the type of individuals who tend to walk a path all their own. Unlike Aries, however, many overlook this quality of Cancer – and are soon shocked when they see the moves Cancer makes.

As a water sign that is symbolized by the crab, Cancers are widely known for their guarded, and sensitive personalities. Their ruler is the moon, which has long been documented across thousands of cultures across many thousands of years as having a visible effect on terrestrial life forms. So much so, in fact, that Lady Luna (the moon) has been associated with lunatics, lunacy, and other forms of psychotic disorder.

Unfortunately, this has contributed to many adopting a poor opinion of emotions in general, and emotional individuals by extension. This in turn colors some opinions of Cancers, who are often teased as the crybabies of the zodiac. Whether or not that's true, the fact is their highly keen sensitivity can be developed into their greatest asset... or devolve into their greatest liability.

## Common Karmic Lessons

"With great power, comes great responsibility", is a popular saying. It describes the Cancer person's predicament perfectly. Cancers are highly intuitive, mentally tough, and possess an inner tenacity that few zodiac signs could rival (Scorpio and Capricorn are some of the exceptions that come to mind).  When their will is directed toward an aim, you'd best get out of their way!

Of course, if success were that easy to achieve, many more would be enjoying their dream life. Cancers unfortunately have had to adapt to a world where people are often ridiculed or punished for their emotions, be they positive or negative expressions. Natural nurturers who act from a place of love, they often become more and more sheltered, introverted, and closed off as they grow older, due to life experiences. Rare is the Cancer who reaches adulthood with their inner sense of freedom fully intact; but, it can be fought for, and brought back.

Like Pisces, Scorpio, and Libra, Cancer is a sign that runs a real risk of over-giving, particularly those who do not appreciate, or reciprocate. This isn't healthy for them, or the people they over-give to, in the long run. One of Cancer's biggest challenges is to learn how to protect and provide to others without smothering them, either physically or energetically.

Similarly, Cancers are notorious for prioritizing security, which often stems from a fear of loss, or a deeply-rooted lack mentality. While their natural sense of thrift is generally beneficial, they get more out of life by not counting every penny, pinching every cent, or hoarding 'til the end of time. Practicing healthy detachment by periodically letting go of unneeded possessions, and traveling to new locations, can help Cancer renew that love of freedom and adventure that so many sacrifice between adolescence and adulthood.

## Karmic Clues by Nodes

Opposite to Cancer is the tenth house ruler, Capricorn. In everyone's birth chart there is a North Node (also known as Rahu), and a South Node (also known as Ketu). The sign our South Node is in speaks to where we're coming from as a sentient soul – or in other words, our recent past lives, and predominant mindsets and skillsets as a result. The sign of our North Node – which is always approximate 180 degrees apart from the South Node, just as Capricorn always rests 180 degrees opposite Cancer – represents the areas of life we are less comfortable in or accustomed to, but will lead to the most growth and fulfillment for the soul, when pursued and developed.

In other words, the South Node sign can be said to reflect the things that come easy to us (our comfort zones), whereas the North Node represents the things that only come with conscious, deliberate effort (our greatest growth opportunities). Understanding the Nodes and their role in our destiny (that is, destination), is vital to understanding our karmic astrology. For Cancer, understanding the Capricorn archetype is just as beneficial as understanding their own Cancerian nature.

If you know you have Cancer as your South Node, you probably will gain even more benefits by reading the Capricorn chapter as well. Pay special attention to your career and work life, as well as your relationship with your father, and reflect on how the latter has helped shape who you are. Consider incorporating S.M.A.R.T. goals into your life.

## Root Karmic Triggers for Cancer

The phrase "root karmic triggers" refers to people, things, and situations that are most likely to reflect or highlight a person's karma from birth, based on their sun sign. Think of them as "sensitive" areas, if you like. These often contain deep vulnerabilities within the psyche of the Cancer archetype, and hide an uncultivated wellspring of great, transcendent power if the appropriate conscious work is put in to transform weakness into strength.

It is highly generalized – no two Cancers are exactly the same, after all – and should be taken with a reasonable grain of salt. However, even with the potential for some margin of error, these triggers may prove to be a common theme for many who identify under the sign of Cancer; even those who may not have their natal sun in Cancer (having moon in Cancer, for example). As a result, it is highly recommended that every Cancer individual examine these areas in their life, and utilize them as opportunities to evolve:

## SEEKING SECURITY

Like the hermit crab clinging to its found shell, Cancers are naturally money-minded, as money equals security – or at least some semblance of it – in a modern capitalist economy. To reiterate: there is nothing wrong with stashing aside a few dollars. However, too many Cancers have a habit of saving and saving for a hypothetical rainy day... yet never taking a moment to actually enjoy the fruits of their labors. Don't forget to come out of that shell every now and again, and see what else life has to offer besides the comforts of the known.

## THE HOME

I've known a great number of outgoing Cancers; but in general, they are typically considered to be among the homebodies of the zodiac. (As always: one's moon, rising,

Mars, and other placements do have a significant effect on a person's persona, whether we consider them or not.) Even if it takes the form of a religious ideal, a strong love bond with another person, a clowder of kittens, or a particular scenic spot outdoors, every Cancer needs to have someone (or something) that feels like home, for inner peace. And if it doesn't exist: build it!

## EVERYONE'S MOTHER

Cancers are unequivocally the mom of the zodiac. Whether male or female, with or without children, they are prone to be providers and protectors of those around them. This sometimes manifests in unhealthy leanings towards controlling or sheltering others. Nobody wants to see the person in front of them fall... but you have to give them enough space to move freely.

## In Short...

The most pressing lesson for sun Cancers – as well as individuals with prominent Cancer birth chart placements – is becoming adept at managing their emotions. I'm not talking about crying, either. (I personally don't get the backlash against tears. Its generally very purifying for the body and mind.)

Emotions contain great power; even moreso when they aren't denied or repressed. By learning how to be fully present in any given moment, and feeling what you feel, you can adopt a state of mind of your choosing, and act or create from that mindset.

Though sometimes branded as odd or quirky, many Cancers are just saddled with inventive minds that view things from a different angle than most. Learn to relish your unique perspective, and use it to create abundance in your life, for you and your loved ones.

While nobody is required to have a family of their own – especially in the 21st century – most Cancers will find that life extremely fulfilling, on a soul level.

If you identify with Cancer, ask yourself the following questions:

1. Why do I hold onto the things I hold on to?

2. What, or where, is home?

3. What am I most fearful of letting go, and why?

Answer these questions honestly, and reflect on each of them afterwards to ascertain where you currently are on your life journey karmically.

# 5

# LEO: PRIDE & DIGNITY

**Affirmation:** "I am magnificent, and display magnanimity, in all my ways."

Leos are not always the most loud or braggadocious, but nearly every single one of them carries a deep sense of self pride inside that burns like a wildfire. In fact, many Leos are known more for their generosity and easygoing demeanor than anything even remotely resembling arrogance.

Those who got it don't need to flaunt it, right? Even so, there is a potential pitfall here that Leos need to be mindful of.

## Common Karmic Lessons

As a fixed sign that is ruled by the sun – yes; that sun – the lion of the zodiac packs a lot of passion, presence, and prestige. And while most are more likely to go out of their way to make others feel comfortable than to parade around with their chest puffed up and out, there can be a tendency for Leos to get rigidly stuck in their views.

Much like Aries, Leos may have a hard time admitting, or even recognizing when they're wrong (especially since they're right more often than not). However, "pride goeth before a fall", so every Leo should do their best to cultivate genuine humility, and learn to truly value and consider input and viewpoints from others.

Similar to an actual cat in heat, Leos are sometimes prone to buckle under the weight of their desires, which sometimes leads to scandals, shame, and other compromising situations. A well-disciplined Leo that is not easily moved is a shining figure of regality that instills confidence and trust. A Leo that is easily swayed by temptation, however, is reduced to a portion of their former glory. Incredible things are made possible by channeling that same sexual energy into other creative endeavors.

## Karmic Clues by Nodes

Opposite to Leo is the eleventh house ruler, Aquarius. In everyone's birth chart there is a North Node (also known as Rahu), and

a South Node (also known as Ketu). The
sign our South Node is in speaks to where
we're coming from as a sentient soul –
or in other words, our recent past lives,
and predominant mindsets and skillsets as
a result. The sign of our North Node –
which is always approximate 180 degrees
apart from the South Node, just as Aquarius
always rests 180 degrees opposite Leo –
represents the areas of life we are less
comfortable in or accustomed to, but will
lead to the most growth and fulfillment for
the soul, when pursued and developed.

In other words, the South Node sign can
be said to reflect the things that come
easy to us (our comfort zones), whereas
the North Node represents the things
that only come with conscious, deliberate
effort (our greatest growth opportunities).
Understanding the Nodes and their role

in our destiny (that is, destination), is vital to understanding our karmic astrology. For Leo, understanding the Aquarius archetype is just as beneficial as understanding their own Leo nature.

If you know you have Leo as your South Node, you probably will gain even more benefits by reading the Aquarius chapter as well. Pay special attention to your personal hobbies, interests, and aptitudes. There may be a hidden, creative career path among them that can make you quite wealthy.

## Root Karmic Triggers for Leo

The phrase "root karmic triggers" refers to people, things, and situations that are most likely to reflect or highlight a person's karma from birth, based on their sun sign. Think of them as "sensitive" areas, if you like. These often contain deep vulnerabilities within the psyche of the Leo archetype, and hide an uncultivated wellspring of great, transcendent power if the appropriate conscious work is put in to transform weakness into strength.

It is highly generalized – no two Leos are exactly the same, after all – and should be taken with a reasonable grain of salt. However, even with the potential for some margin of error, these triggers may prove to be a common theme for many who identify under the sign of Leo; even those who may not have their natal sun in Leo (such as a Leo rising, for example).

As a result, it is highly recommended that every Leo individual examine these areas in their life, and utilize them as opportunities to evolve:

## CREATIVE EXPRESSION

It's not hard for Leos to stand out and shine. Leo is the actor or performer of the zodiac, as they naturally tend to appreciate drawing the eyes of others. Even the quiet and withdrawn among them most likely excel in some area or talent, especially where the arts are concerned. (Perhaps they'd be more at home behind the scenes, in the director's chair?)

They don't have to make money from their passion pursuits, but that's the path of most prosperity for Leos in general. If nothing else, having something in their lives they can enjoy just for its own sake of self-expression is essential. For Leos who settle into an employee role, it is vital that they feel like a valued asset on the team for their mental health.

## LEADING WITH PRIDE

You can learn a lot about a Leo by how they present themselves to the world. Never let a Leo fool you about where they stand here: every single one of them has a high opinion of themselves. I don't care what their socioeconomic status is, or their level of accolades or education; rare is the Leo who does not possess, at the core of their being, an unshakeable sense of pride.

I've known Leos who were in abusive relationships, and you'd never know it from how they presented themselves on the surface. It's not that they are immune to conditions like anxiety, doubts or depressions. It's just that in spite of all that, there is no force on Earth capable of completing silencing a lion's true roar.

That being said, every Leo should take great care that pride and self-confidence don't distort into blind arrogance or narcissism. They tend to work against their own best interests at that point.

## WHERE THE HEART IS

Leos are secretly big softies, who love the warmth provided by big happy families, and good company. Authenticity is important to them, so they tend to prefer a tight inner circle over a gang of contacts to keep up with. By cultivating their closest relationships (platonic and familial), Leos will expand their rather massive heart space, and in turn, radiate a pure light that attracts and sustains those around them... much like their ruler, the sun.

## In Short...

The most pressing lesson for sun Leos
– as well as individuals with prominent
Leo birth chart placements – is two-fold:
confidence, and creative self-expression.
The former must be free of any false
sense of over-inflated self-importance. The
latter must be honest and true to the Leos
character, or the passion will perish.

Leos tend to build upon a strong foundation
of knowledge over the years, and provided
there is maturity, will often have a solid
bedrock of wisdom to show for it. With their
ample repository of anecdotes and stories,
they tend to make great godparents and
grandparents.

If there are no children in your life, consider
volunteering at places where you can
interact with some, such as coaching a
team, or attending a reading room in a

public library, for example. Few things in life can light up a Leo as brightly as the bold smiles and unfiltered laughter of children.

If you identify with Leo, ask yourself the following questions:

1. Is my self-image determined by myself, or present conditions (including others' opinions)?

2. What brings me the most joy on this earth?

3. In what ways am I building on my personal knowledge?

Answer these questions honestly, and reflect on each of them afterwards to ascertain where you currently are on your life journey from a karma-clearing perspective.

# 6

# VIRGO: Purpose & Service

**Affirmation:** "I am a blessing in the lives of others with generous acts of service."

The virgin of the zodiac is also one of its most enigmatic and mysterious characters. "Mysterious" is probably not a word you've often seen used to describe these graceful individuals; but there are many levels and layers to a Virgo. The thing is, the average onlooker or acquaintance won't get close enough to see them.

## Common Karmic Lessons

Like Gemini, Virgo is mutable, and ruled by quicksilver Mercury. However, Virgo is a feminine earth sign. As a result, they tend to be a little more reserved in sharing their outlooks and opinions, and are often more inclined to play a background or supportive role, as to being front and center.

This has nothing to do with Virgo's leadership capabilities. Far from it. The truth is, most Virgos severely underestimate themselves, and to a degree that nobody outside themselves would. Some are more confident and outgoing than others; in most cases, the more bold among them built up that level of assertiveness over many years and lessons along the way.

Some of this can be attributed to the natural modalities of Virgo. If we translated each sign of the zodiac into one of the popular love languages, then Virgo would undoubtedly be "acts of service". Of all the signs (although followed closely by Pisces), Virgo is most attuned to finding fulfillment and purpose through service. This can be a family, an occupation, or a community: but to be of use lives in their core.

As admirable a quality as this is, it can have a debilitating effect for an unbalanced Virgo. Like other earth signs, they can easily run the risk of overworking their bodies or minds, developing poor eating habits, and potentially burning out. They will work harder, longer, and consistently, without a complaint or any desire to abandon the task. These tendencies can lead to two additional dangers: of the Virgo expecting too much of themselves, and of others taking advantage of their consideration and generosity.

## Karmic Clues by Nodes

Opposite to Virgo is the twelfth house ruler, Pisces. In everyone's birth chart there is a North Node (also known as Rahu), and a South Node (also known as Ketu). The sign our South Node is in speaks to where we're coming from as a sentient soul – or in other words, our recent past lives, and predominant mindsets and skillsets as a result. The sign of our North Node – which is always approximate 180 degrees apart from the South Node, just as Pisces always rests 180 degrees opposite Virgo – represents the areas of life we are less comfortable in or accustomed to, but will lead to the most growth and fulfillment for the soul, when pursued and developed.

In other words, the South Node sign can be said to reflect the things that come easy to us (our comfort zones), whereas the North Node represents the things that only come with conscious, deliberate effort (our greatest growth opportunities). Understanding the Nodes and their role in our destiny (that is, destination), is vital to understanding our karmic astrology. For Virgo, understanding the Pisces archetype is just as beneficial as understanding their own Virgo nature.

If you know you have Virgo as your South Node, you probably will gain even more benefits by reading the Pisces chapter as well. Pay special attention to areas in life where you have a tendency to give too much of yourself! Also take note of the importance of religion/spirituality for your well-being.

## Root Karmic Triggers for Virgo

The phrase "root karmic triggers" refers to people, things, and situations that are most likely to reflect or highlight a person's karma from birth, based on their sun sign. Think of them as "sensitive" areas, if you like. These often contain deep vulnerabilities within the psyche of the Virgo archetype, and hide an uncultivated wellspring of great, transcendent power if the appropriate conscious work is put in to transform weakness into strength.

It is highly generalized – no two Virgos are exactly the same, after all – and should be taken with a reasonable grain of salt. However, even with the potential for some margin of error, these triggers may prove to be a common theme for many who identify under the sign of Virgo; even those who may not have their natal sun in Virgo (such as a moon in Virgo, for example). As a result, it is highly recommended that every Virgo individual examine these areas in their life, and utilize them as opportunities to evolve:

## GIVING AND RECEIVING

Like Libra, and Pisces, Virgos can have a tendency to give too much to others, while giving too little to themselves. Too much time; too much attention; too much money; too much everything. In these instances, their charitable nature gets the best of them. By setting healthy boundaries, and respecting physical limitations, Virgos can build more reciprocal relationships in their lives without demanding it. Lessening the pressure they like to place on themselves can also soften the voice of that harsh and misleading inner critic that incessantly barks in their head.

## HEALTH IS WEALTH

Virgo rules the sixth house of health and mundane matters, as well as the digestive tract. It is not uncommon for Virgos to suffer from digestion problems when something in their life is out of order. Their ruling planet of Mercury also places great emphasis on their mental processes and analytical abilities, which are quite impressive... but also at risk.

If Virgo doesn't take care to keep stress levels low and allow themselves adequate time to recharge and renew, it could lead to future complications such as brain aneurysms.

## A ROUTINE LIFE

Virgos can tolerable, and even enjoy, a regular daily routine more than many. Still, adding a little magic and spice to mundane obligations will go a long way to boost a Virgo's productivity and inner calm. Since the Virgo mind never truly powers down, their next best bet is to at least learn how to operate it on a softer setting. This is where healthy "distractions & detours" come into play.

**In Short...**

The most pressing lesson for sun Virgos – as well as individuals with prominent Virgo birth chart placements – is to learn to balance work, health, and happiness. Setting realistic expectations, maintaining a practical schedule that doesn't demand superhuman levels of productivity out of them, and sprinkling in some "me-time" will lead to a very satisfied Virgo.

Virgos can achieve great heights in life if they can learn to prioritize their needs first. As selfish as that may sound, it really isn't, especially when it's pertaining to Virgo. As they are predisposed to tending to others, adopting more of a self-centered framework actually has the opposite effect of producing a narcissistic person.

Rather, it helps balance them out, preventing them from over-giving and over-doing for others, who will in turn learn to value and appreciate who Virgo is and what Virgo does even more.

Unlike some signs such as Leo, Sagittarius or Aries, Virgos can thrive and flourish in even the most menial types of work. They do equally well in trade or creative pursuits, giving them a variety of options with which to make their worldly contributions. Whichever occupation or career they do decide upon, as long as the Virgo feels and knows that they are making a positive difference, their soul will blossom.

If you identify with Virgo, ask yourself the following questions:

1. Do I speak kind thoughts to myself?

2. How am I influenced by other people's expectations?

3. When was the last time I did something enjoyable, just for me?

Answer each question honestly, and reflect on them afterwards to determine how you are currently progressing on your karmic journey.

# 7

# LIBRA: Both Sides

**Affirmation:** "I am not afraid to let my light shine, and inspire others to do the same."

As the only sign that is represented by neither animal nor man, Libras can't help but to stand out. Whether in the home, out in public, or at the workplace, the Libra will find it difficult to not make an impression on others (whether positive or not).

The 7th sign of the zodiac brings with it an overall shift from the self, towards others (or the collective). This shift carries with it a host of new challenges, tests, and potential to evolve.

## Common Karmic Lessons

Libra is a masculine air sign, and the 3rd cardinal following Cancer and Aries. With Venus as a ruler, they are naturally geared towards communications, relating to others, and all forms of the arts and aesthetics. Their symbol is the scales of justice, but this doesn't imply that Libra is balanced. In many cases, far from it!

While the average Libra is skilled at giving the appearance of being in balance, we all know that things are not always as they appear. In reality, most Libras find themselves in a seemingly endless back-and-forth of being up and down, high and low, fearless... and fearful.

Libras are also often considered indecisive, or people-pleasers. While both of these traits will be far less prevalent in a mature Libra, the root remains – and it stems from a sound place. As the scales, Libras are naturally able to see multiple sides to any situation, even beyond their own perceptions and beliefs.

It's a powerful ability worth harnessing, but if neglected or misused, it can create an imbalance within the individual leading to restlessness and unreliability. And before they know it, the Libra has built up a false persona controlled by the need to keep everyone around them content, at the cost of their own authenticity and autonomy. A false peace, is no peace at all.

## Karmic Clues by Nodes

Opposite to Libra is the first house ruler, Aries. In everyone's birth chart there is a North Node (also known as Rahu), and a South Node (also known as Ketu). The sign our South Node is in speaks to where we're coming from as a sentient soul – or in other words, our recent past lives, and predominant mindsets and skillsets as a result. The sign of our North Node – which is always approximate 180 degrees apart from the South Node, just as Aries always rests 180 degrees opposite Libra – represents the areas of life we are less comfortable in or accustomed to, but will lead to the most growth and fulfillment for the soul, when pursued and developed.

In other words, the South Node sign can be said to reflect the things that come easy to us (our comfort zones), whereas the North Node represents the things that only come with conscious, deliberate effort (our greatest growth opportunities). Understanding the Nodes and their role in our destiny (that is, destination), is vital to understanding our karmic astrology. For Libra, understanding the Aries archetype is just as beneficial as understanding their own Libran nature.

If you know you have Libra as your South Node, you probably will gain even more benefits by reading the Aries chapter as well. Pay special attention to how you compete with others, as well as how you approach leadership roles. Do you rise to the occasion, or slink into the shadows so as not to stand out or stir the pot?

## Root Karmic Triggers for Libra

The phrase "root karmic triggers" refers to people, things, and situations that are most likely to reflect or highlight a person's karma from birth, based on their sun sign. Think of them as "sensitive" areas, if you like. These often contain deep vulnerabilities within the psyche of the Libra archetype, and hide an uncultivated wellspring of great, transcendent power if the appropriate conscious work is put in to transform weakness into strength.

It is highly generalized – no two Libras are exactly the same, after all – and should be taken with a reasonable grain of salt. However, even with the potential for some margin of error, these triggers may prove to be a common theme for many who identify under the sign of Libra; even those who may not have their natal sun in Libra (such as a moon in Libra, for example). As a result, it is highly recommended that every Libra individual examine these areas in their life, and utilize them as opportunities to evolve:

## PEOPLE-PLEASING PARADOX

Libras love people, platonically and passionately. Their love at times can lead them astray though, if they are not relating to others from a frame of self-respect and self-awareness. The main problem with indiscriminately putting others first, is that it isn't based in grace or charity, but pity. As a result, the Libra's sense of self will inevitably suffer.

Setting healthy boundaries can be a struggle for a hopeless romantic heart like most Libras. With Venus influencing them heavily, they sometimes place too much emphasis on external appearances, and can struggle with maintaining the same. Venus also bestows upon Libra a love of all forms of pleasure, which can take unfortunate turns in laziness, gluttony, or lust if discipline isn't practiced.

## TAKING ACTION

Libras are very capable movers and shakers, but many of them develop a tendency to avoid acting in a manner that might isolate them from others. The mind of a Libra is a place rife with potential and possibility. How many of these possibilities come to fruition? Typically, not many. Many Libras suffer in silence needlessly due to a tendency to hold themselves back from taking action in life.

An example of this is a Libra in a work meeting where the supervisor is asking for a volunteer to lead a team for a special project. The Libra might know they are more than qualified for the role, and the others would follow their leadership, but the Libra will sit back and let someone else take the spot, even if they're not best suited to the task at hand.

The happiest Libras are those that honor the insights and visions they receive, make up their mind, and move forward.

## JUDGE & JURY

The ability to see many sides of situations brings with it the potential for one of the more harsh traits of a Libra: their judgment. Since they are more able than most to view things from many angles, they may take a minute to decide where they stand on a matter – but once they do, they tend to stand firm. At the same time, they tend to convince themselves that their judgments are correct and impartial, even when they're not. This can lead some Libras to think they're always right (although you'll have a tough time finding one who would admit that).

## In Short...

The most pressing lesson for sun Libras – as well as any individual with prominent Libra birth chart placements – is to first both acknowledge and accept themselves, without requiring any approval, or validation, from others.

It is only after a Libra has learned to love themselves, from the inside out, that they expect to attract the kind of partners that will prove lasting & beneficial in their lives, whether the partnership in question be pertaining to friendship, business, or intimate. By the same token, it will benefit them to accept people for who they are, where they are, as opposed to who they could be.

As a sign ruled by Venus, Libras are naturally magnetic. However, so long as they undermine their individuality and silence their voice for the sake of "keeping the peace", their own magnetism will be operating at a lower frequency, and this will be reflected by the quality of the people places and things that they will be drawn to... and find drawn to them.

Once a Libra learns to fully embrace their cardinal quality as a born leader and troubadour, there will be no end to the good in life that they will attract without effort.

If you identify with Libra, ask yourself the following questions:

1. What is my relationship with myself

like?

2. Who comes first in life?

3. What's more important: avoiding conflict, or seeking solutions?

Answer these questions honestly, and reflect on each of them afterwards to ascertain where you currently are on your life journey karmically.

# 8

# SCORPIO: THE REINCARNATOR

**Affirmation:** "I am more powerful than even I know, and will triumph over all hardships."

Most frequently associated with the scorpion, Scorpio has also been symbolized in times past as the serpent, the lizard, the spider, the wolf, the eagle, and at its apex: the phoenix. (I've even read one source that included the otter and rabbit in the mix, interestingly enough.) The phoenix was thought to represent a mature Scorpio who had evolved beyond the lower levels of behavior.

Talk to a passing Scorpio on the street, and ask them to share their life story with you. Chances are you'll wish you'd picked up some popcorn first. Many Scorpios shoulder a staggering amount of tribulations in their lifetime, to the extent that some develop the erroneous idea that stress and suffering are unavoidable elements of our reality.

Those who resist succumbing to that abyss, will eventually rise from the ashes of their past like the legendary phoenix, and attain heights the previous versions of them seldom dared dream.

## Common Karmic Lessons

Scorpio is a fixed water feminine sign, whose still waters run deep. You may think you know a Scorpio. I guarantee you: you do not. Most Scorpios don't even fully know themselves! Not for quite a long time at least. Scorpios tend to be less intimidated by the idea of death, because of the way life events play out for them.

Perhaps it has something to do with the effect their planetary ruler Mars has, but Scorpios can feel as if they've lived several lifetimes in one with all the upheavals and personal transformations they tend to undergo. While some shifts are more pleasant than others, they always demand that the old Scorpio die, and a new Scorpio rise in its place.

This all-or-nothing quality carries over into all areas of a Scorpio's life. When they are all in, they are all the way in. Whether this takes the form of putting in a work all-nighter, or showing their love partner total devotion and surrender... it takes a lot to get a Scorpio to that place, but once they arrive, they demonstrate a fixated determination that rivals any tunnel vision you've seen.

This "all-in" mindset can easily backfire in many situations. For Scorpios to make the most of their untapped potential, adopting a balanced mindset that practices boundaries, and honors the practical as well as the optimistic, will take them far.

## Karmic Clues by Nodes

Opposite to Scorpio is the second house ruler, Taurus. In everyone's birth chart there is a North Node (also known as Rahu), and a South Node (also known as Ketu). The sign our South Node is in speaks to where we're coming from as a sentient soul

– or in other words, our recent past lives, and predominant mindsets and skillsets as a result. The sign of our North Node – which is always approximate 180 degrees apart from the South Node, just as Taurus always rests 180 degrees opposite Scorpio – represents the areas of life we are less comfortable in or accustomed to, but will lead to the most growth and fulfillment for the soul, when pursued and developed.

In other words, the South Node sign can be said to reflect the things that come easy to us (our comfort zones), whereas the North Node represents the things that only come with conscious, deliberate effort (our greatest growth opportunities). Understanding the Nodes and their role in our destiny (that is, destination), is vital to understanding our karmic astrology. For Scorpio, understanding the

Taurus archetype is just as beneficial as understanding their own Scorpio nature.

If you know you have Scorpio as your South Node, you probably will gain even more benefits by reading the Taurus chapter as well. Pay special attention to how you manage your assets and resources. Avoid people and habits that tend to put your sense of stability at risk.

## Root Karmic Triggers for Scorpio

The phrase "root karmic triggers" refers to people, things, and situations that are most likely to reflect or highlight a person's karma from birth, based on their sun sign. Think of them as "sensitive" areas, if you like. These often contain deep vulnerabilities within the psyche of the Scorpio archetype, and hide an uncultivated wellspring of great, transcendent power if the appropriate conscious work is put in to transform weakness into strength.

It is highly generalized – no two Scorpios are exactly the same, after all – and should be taken with a reasonable grain of salt. However, even with the potential for some margin of error, these triggers may prove to be a common theme for many who identify under the sign of Scorpio; even those who may not have their natal sun in Scorpio (such as a Scorpio rising, for example). As a result, it is highly recommended that every Scorpio individual examine these areas in their life, and utilize them as opportunities to evolve:

## SEXUAL ENERGY

Scorpio is the sign associated with the reproductive organs. This fact, along with their tendency to be effortlessly alluring and mysterious, only adds to the mystique that is often attributed to them. Many might be disappointed to know that despite their strong sexual aura, many Scorpios are not highly sexually active. I myself have known several Scorpios as an adult who were long-time celibates by choice.

When it comes to the urge to merge, Scorpios typically fall into either one of two camps: the "gotta-have-its", and the alchemists. The gottas will play the game, claim their "kills", and repeat the cycle. They simply love the act itself. For them, there is almost no experience on earth that compares to the feelings two separate beings can create by bridging their bodies.

The alchemists tend to be more reserved with their intimacy, preferring to transmute that powerful energy into other areas to reap its benefits. This doesn't mean that these types of Scorpios are always chaste or virgins, or even practicing abstinence. They just aren't so quick to share that sublime experience with just any and everyone, especially when the passion is driven by shallow or superficial attraction.

## ACCEPTING PAIN

As is often the case, Scorpio's strengths can easily become weaknesses. In particular, the Scorpio's high pain tolerance. A Scorpio can be lied to, betrayed, evicted, abandoned, and fired from their job – all in the same day. And they will still wake up the next day.

Part of the Scorpio's journey is learning to overcome all setbacks, never giving up, and always transforming into the version of them they need to be right now. While this iron will to persevere can be commendable, it can also produce in too many Scorpios a habit of confusing pain with pleasure.

A Scorpio who grows too accustomed to suffering, or stares too long into the abyss, may find themselves embracing too much of their shadow qualities, and neglect most of their inner light.

## HEALTHY BOUNDARIES

The penchant for pain acceptance ties back into the Scorpio's personal relationships as well. Even though they can be known for being vengeful and cutthroat when they want to be (though practicing gratitude and forgiveness will bring them more favorable results), the average Scorpio is far more likely to turn both cheeks and take the hits.

Scorpios are far more romantic and clingy than many have been led to believe. When a Scorpio gives someone their heart, they give it all – and this can come back to bite if they placed their trust in the wrong person or people. It is imperative that Scorpios learn how to set the proper parameters in their relationships, so that there is no resentment or neglect in the future.

## In Short...

The most pressing lesson for sun Scorpio – as well as individuals with prominent Scorpio birth chart placements – is to learn how to live away from the razor's edge. Being able to turn even the largest mountain of lemons into lemonade is useful, sure. But, is it always necessary? Is it always efficient? Is it always what's called for?

I'll say it again: practicing gratitude and forgiveness will do wonders for Scorpio in the long run. As a water sign, it is sometimes all too easy for them to sink into the depths of their emotions. Adopting more positive attitudes towards the situations they find themselves in will help raise their vibration, and present them with additional opportunities in life.

The biggest challenge for the Scorpio, ultimately, is to not self-destruct. Instead: re-construct. This is the mission; should Scorpio choose to accept it.

If you identify with Scorpio, ask yourself the following questions:

1. In what ways do I self-sabotage?

2. When others hurt me deeply, what is my response?

3. What in life am I tolerating, and why?

Answer these questions honestly, and reflect on each of them afterwards to ascertain where you currently are on your life journey from a karma-clearing perspective.

# 9

# SAGITTARIUS: DREAMS UNLIMITED

**Affirmation:** "I am always ready to learn, and then share, what life has to teach."

Sagittarius, the centaur and archer, is one of the most fun-loving signs, but don't let that fool you. When it comes to engaging in philosophical debates, or challenging commonly-held notions of the nature of reality, this Jupiter-ruled person can go toe-to-toe with a deep-thinking Scorpio, or a far-reaching Aquarius.

Being generally well-built individuals, Sagittarians have a love for physical activity that rivals their scholastic interests. Naturally some will lean more towards the intellectual and others towards the athletic, but every Sagittarius will reap benefits by adopting a more temperate approach to daily life that exercises both mind and body.

## Common Karmic Lessons

The ninth sign of Sagittarius is a mutable fire sign that is ruled by benevolent Jupiter. Every person is born free, but a Sagittarius will tend to retain this quality longer than most. One stereotype often reserved for them is their luck, which many consider to be to an unfair degree. I don't know how much "luckier" a Sagittarius is compared to the next, but I'm sure their generally optimistic nature that views anything as possible certainly doesn't hurt.

We all have to touch down on earth feet-first at some point, however. Sagittarians can go farther and achieve more in life by learning to prioritize balancing both sides of their nature: the higher self, and the lower self. The version of them that loves books and learning, and the version of them that adores exploring the outdoors and seeing the world. Neither side should be placed above the other; and that is where their greatest test lies.

Another potential pitfall of their upbeat, go-go-go demeanor is it can lead to direct talks, unfiltered words, and the hurt feelings of others who aren't used to blunt speech. It's very unusual for a Sagittarius to be deliberately mean-spirited towards another unprovoked... but that doesn't mean their words can't hurt. A mature Sagittarian interested in evolving will learn to respect the feelings of others, and not blindly say what is on their mind without any regard of the other person.

## Karmic Clues by Nodes

Opposite to Sagittarius is the third house ruler, Gemini. In everyone's birth chart there is a North Node (also known as Rahu), and a South Node (also known as Ketu). The sign our South Node is in speaks to where we're coming from as a sentient soul – or in other words, our recent past lives, and predominant mindsets and skillsets as a result. The sign of our North Node – which is always approximate 180 degrees apart from the South Node, just as Gemini always rests 180 degrees opposite Sagittarius –

represents the areas of life we are less comfortable in or accustomed to, but will lead to the most growth and fulfillment for the soul, when pursued and developed.

In other words, the South Node sign can be said to reflect the things that come easy to us (our comfort zones), whereas the North Node represents the things that only come with conscious, deliberate effort (our greatest growth opportunities). Understanding the Nodes and their role in our destiny (that is, destination), is vital to understanding our karmic astrology. For Sagittarius, understanding the Gemini archetype is just as beneficial as understanding their own Sagittarian nature.

If you know you have Sagittarius as your South Node, you probably will gain even more benefits by reading the Gemini chapter as well. Pay special attention to how you socialize: how you respond to others, and how they respond to you. How much time do you spend considering opinions and views that don't match your own?

## Root Karmic Triggers for Sagittarius

The phrase "root karmic triggers" refers to people, things, and situations that are most likely to reflect or highlight a person's karma from birth, based on their sun sign. Think of them as "sensitive" areas, if you like. These often contain deep vulnerabilities within the psyche of the Sagittarius archetype, and hide an uncultivated wellspring of great, transcendent power if the appropriate conscious work is put in to transform weakness into strength.

It is highly generalized – no two Sagittarians are exactly the same, after all – and should be taken with a reasonable grain of salt. However, even with the potential for some margin of error, these triggers may prove to be a common theme for many who identify under the sign of Sagittarius; even those who may not have their natal sun in Sagittarius (such as a Mars in Sagittarius, for example). As a result, it is highly recommended that every Sagittarius individual examine these areas in their life, and utilize them as opportunities to evolve:

## MIND-BODY BALANCE

This is arguably the most critical cheat code for Sagittarius to unlock a better life for themselves. Devote time to develop both body and mind, and Sagittarius will prove to be a force to be reckoned with (and hopefully, a force for good). For the mind, play chess. Read the works of the great writers of old, as well as modern-day classics. Engage in legos, arts and crafts, or puzzle games.

For the body, meditate. Get into yoga or tai-chi. Exercise regularly. Eat to live. Breathe fresh air. Get a good bike ride, jog, or hike in here and there.

## TEMPERANCE & DOGMATISM

Despite coming off as open-minded most of the time, a Sagittarius can be surprisingly dogmatic when it comes to personal beliefs. Even those that aren't particularly religious can have a set of beliefs that they would go to conversational war over. If this applies to you, adopt an attitude of acceptance towards others.

As wise and sage as a Sagittarius can be, they do well to keep their ego out of that picture. We are all different people having different experiences, so it is only natural that some, if not all of our views are different as well. That's no reason to clash or come into conflict. Take these opportunities to see where the commonalities lie between you and other people. Emphasize that unites, not what divides.

## DREAMS COMING TRUE

Like Pisces and Aries, Sagittarius is one of the biggest dreamers among the zodiac. They aim high – higher than most – and they may doubt themselves or have second thoughts if they share their aspirations with less imaginative individuals. (Or: they can say "screw them", and go for it anyway; a perfectly Sagittarian response.)

When it comes to rapid brainstorms and flash-in-the-pan ideas, few match the output of the idea factory that is Sagittarius. It can be tough keeping track of all that inspiration, and even tougher bringing them to life. It's recommended that these individuals keep a journal nearby at all times, so they never risk losing that next great idea that might change the world – or at the very least, theirs.

**In Short...**

The most pressing lesson for sun Sagittarius – as well as individuals with prominent Sagittarius birth chart placements – is one of tolerance, and acceptance. Balancing the mental and physical forces at play within them will also produce the added benefit of leveling out their temperament, which can run hot at times. Sagittarians have a mighty war cry, and they need to use it wisely.

The perpetual dreamers, Sagittarians should never be afraid to go after their wildest dreams, no matter how unusual or lofty they may seem. It could be long-term, such a forging a new career path; or short-term, like touching the Grand Canyon or the Great Wall. Whatever it is: write it down, visualize it, and go over the steps it'll take to make it happen.

And remember: there's no rule that says you can only have one dream. And once it's been achieved, be sure to share the wisdom and knowledge you obtained along your journey with the rest of the world.

If you identify with Sagittarius, ask yourself the following questions:

1. What areas of life am I ignoring or neglecting?

2. How do my words make others feel?

3. When's the last time I brought one of my dreams to life?

Answer each question honestly, and reflect on them afterwards to determine how you are currently progressing on your karmic journey.

# 10

# CAPRICORN: THE BUSY BODY

**Affirmation:** "I am the architect of my physical reality."

The winter solstice in the West ushers in the brisk cold, which find their match in Saturn-ruled Capricorn. This is not to say the zodiac symbolized by the mythical sea goat is overly cold or harsh. (Well; they can be.) What it means is, Capricorns have a knack for overcoming great odds and obstacles that would have left lesser individuals broken and battered versions of themselves... and they'll smile while doing it.

This desire to succeed comes with its shadow side – namely: the willingness to do whatever it takes to attain it. (For those aware of the Watergate scandal involving U.S. president Richard Nixon: he was a sun Capricorn.) Capricorns should never sacrifice their ethics and values for material gains, or it's only a matter of time until those gains become losses.

## Common Karmic Lessons

The tenth sign of the zodiac is all about making things happen in the material world. As the final cardinal sign, Capricorns are known for being self-starters and prone towards excellence. They also aren't too self-absorbed to ignore what works from others, and are not above adapting tested methods and practices into their own routines and workflows. For Capricorn: "if it ain't broke, build on it."

Despite being one of the feminine signs, Capricorns can be quite comfortable in expressing their masculine energy, and are generally among the most ambitious and worldly people. Their ruler Saturn endows them with the powers of patience, planning, and perseverance. Saturn's rule can be quite stern though, and also comes with delays, disappointments, and bouts of depression. It is essential for the sake of a Capricorn's long-term health and happiness that they cultivate more humor and simple joys in their lives.

Capricorns often have a silly, even goofy side to them that not everyone is privileged to witness. Since they place so much importance on making it in the world, they are very cautious about how they present themselves to others. They are not the type to wear their heart on their sleeve, or speak their mind freely, unless they are with trusted company, or sitting in a position of power. (And even then, that's a maybe.) Work and career can have a disproportionate amount of importance in their lives, causing other areas to suffer.

## Karmic Clues by Nodes

Opposite to Capricorn is the fourth house ruler, Cancer. In everyone's birth chart there is a North Node (also known as Rahu), and a South Node (also known as Ketu). The sign our South Node is in speaks to where we're coming from as a sentient soul – or in other words, our recent past lives, and predominant mindsets and skillsets as

a result. The sign of our North Node –
which is always approximate 180 degrees
apart from the South Node, just as
Cancer always rests 180 degrees opposite
Capricorn – represents the areas of life
we are less comfortable in or accustomed
to, but will lead to the most growth and
fulfillment for the soul, when pursued and
developed.

In other words, the South Node sign can
be said to reflect the things that come
easy to us (our comfort zones), whereas
the North Node represents the things
that only come with conscious, deliberate
effort (our greatest growth opportunities).
Understanding the Nodes and their role
in our destiny (that is, destination),
is vital to understanding our karmic
astrology. For Capricorn, understanding
the Cancer archetype is just as beneficial

as understanding their own Capricornian nature.

If you know you have Capricorn as your South Node, you probably will gain even more benefits by reading the Cancer chapter as well. Pay special attention to your family dynamics, especially with your parents, and your spouse and children, if it applies. Are you giving everyone an appropriate amount of quality time, attention, and care?

## Root Karmic Triggers for Capricorn

The phrase "root karmic triggers" refers to people, things, and situations that are most likely to reflect or highlight a person's karma from birth, based on their sun sign. Think of them as "sensitive" areas, if you like. These often contain deep vulnerabilities within the psyche of the Capricorn archetype, and hide an uncultivated wellspring of great, transcendent power if the appropriate conscious work is put in to transform weakness into strength.

It is highly generalized – no two Capricorns are exactly the same, after all – and should be taken with a reasonable grain of salt. However, even with the potential for some margin of error, these triggers may prove to be a common theme for many who identify under the sign of Capricorn; even those who may not have their natal sun in Capricorn (such as a Venus in Capricorn, for example). As a result, it is highly recommended that every Capricorn individual examine these areas in their life, and utilize them as opportunities to evolve:

## WORK VS LABOR

Capricorn is the natural ruler of the tenth house of the zodiac wheel, which governs work, career, and one's public status and image. And it goes without saying that this area of life tends to take center stage in the drama that is the Capricorn's life. "Work-life balance" is a phrase that had to have been either invented by a Capricorn, or for Capricorns. They're generally resistant to burn out no matter how diligently they exert themselves, but the risk of neglecting other areas of life still runs high. Many family units have suffered and splintered due to the inexhaustible workhorse in their midst.

## NEEDING CONTROL

Capricorns ought to take care not to become control freaks. The reality is, there is very little in our lives that we can physically control – including who gets to wake up tomorrow. The sooner this lesson is learned and accepted, the better. By that same token, a Capricorn ought to honestly examine their friendships and ask themselves if the relationship is based on real camaraderie, or manipulating them in some way for personal gain. It's not unheard of for Capricorns to befriend someone for potential status-based benefits in the future.

## THE FATHER

If Cancers are the mother, then Capricorn is the father. Strict, like a disciplinarian; and often stoic as well. Capricorns can offset any tendencies to unintentionally come off too harshly by spending some time getting to know their inner child. What dreams did the child version of you have? And where are those dreams now? Were they achieved, abandoned, or forgotten altogether?

## In Short...

The most pressing lesson for sun Capricorns – as well as individuals with prominent Capricorn birth chart placements – is to let go of the need to control everything, and to take life a bit more easy at times. The drive to climb new heights in work or status tends to promote an unsavory habit of having to keep things in their boxes and borders, where Capricorn can keep it all in line. Let life breathe. Don't make the mistake of sacrificing the things that most matter in life for the fickle and fleeting.

There's nothing wrong with desiring to build something with a foundation – something that lasts; a legacy worthy of passing down, even. Just don't get carried away by being so focused on the end goal, that you miss the chance to enjoy the journey that was taken to get there. Also keep in mind that nobody in this world achieves anything all on their own. Show appreciation for the people and relationships that have enriched your life, and made all the effort worth a damn.

If you identify with Capricorn, ask yourself the following questions:

1. What am I responsible for, and what am I not?

2. Am I setting aside enough time for the people I love?

3. When was the last time I did

**absolutely** nothing, and enjoyed it?

Answer these questions honestly, and reflect on each of them afterwards to ascertain where you currently are on your life journey karmically.

# 11

# AQUARIUS: TOWARDS THE COLLECTIVE

**Affirmation:** "I am an unfiltered vessel for truth and knowledge that reaches beyond borders."

As an air sign, and one of the few zodiac signs that is represented by a person, Aquarius is intricately tied to the mental world where thoughts dictate what's real. As the eleventh sign, they symbolically embody all of the karmic knowledge that was learned by the previous 10 signs. This culminates in a persona that is deeply invested in what has been called the collective consciousness.

Many Aquarians have a nagging sense that "something is wrong with this picture". One of their greatest desires is to see sweeping change that raises the level of consciousness across the entire planet. Aquarius represents a transition further from the lower man, and closer towards the higher man; from the carnal, to the conscious.

Many Aquarians convey a sense of sovereignty and self-awareness that shows great interest in the direction society as a whole is progressing. Nevertheless, they too, along with every sign, and indeed every individual who has manifested in the third dimension with flesh and blood, have some lessons to learn yet...

## Common Karmic Lessons

In modern astrology, Uranus is typically assigned to be the ruler of Aquarius. In traditional, Saturn is considered their ruler. Uranus is often attributed to Aquarians due to the characteristics of innovation and upheaval associated with both. Aquarians are known for sticking out like a sore thumb in their communities, for one reason or another. They may be exceptionally tall; they may sport facial features that almost appear extra-terrestrial. They might have shocking views that clash with the status quo, or they may tend to steer towards society's outcasts and misfits; and so on.

Saturn's influence on them reinforces the fact that Aquarius is a fixed sign. As a masculine air sign, this creates a sort of internal pressure that manifests in several ways. For one, an Aquarius is far more aware of time than the average person; but not in an obsessive way, and not necessarily time as it appears on a clock. It comes naturally to them – an internal clock that they follow and observe. Some Aquarians are punctual to a fault, while others show up as it suits them. Understand this: no matter the Aquarius, they have a sense of rhythm and time that is internal to them... and they keep it.

While Libra is the air sign most accused of being indecisive, it is a common occurrence to all air signs, including the bearer of water. This is due to an Aquarius' fixed nature, which causes them to tend to cling tightly to their perspective and views. This is at odds with their fondness for observing others and learning new beliefs, which they often disagree with, even if they appear agreeable to others on the surface.

The clearest indication of whether an Aquarius is truly on the same page as another person can generally be determined by how much talking and opening up they do around them. Most of the time, an Aquarius would rather kick back and let others speak their mind, while reserving their true feelings from their lofty seat in the skies. More than anything, the Aquarius desires an experience with others that can be called a true connection; however it might manifest.

## Karmic Clues by Nodes

Opposite to Aquarius is the fifth house ruler, Leo. In everyone's birth chart there is a North Node (also known as Rahu), and a South Node (also known as Ketu). The sign our South Node is in speaks to where we're coming from as a sentient soul – or in other words, our recent past lives, and predominant mindsets and skillsets as a result. The sign of our North Node – which is always approximate 180 degrees apart from the South Node, just as Leo always rests 180 degrees opposite Aquarius – represents the areas of life we are less comfortable in or accustomed to, but will lead to the most growth and fulfillment for the soul, when pursued and developed.

In other words, the South Node sign can be said to reflect the things that come easy to us (our comfort zones), whereas the North Node represents the things that only come with conscious, deliberate effort (our greatest growth opportunities). Understanding the Nodes and their role in our destiny (that is, destination), is vital to understanding our karmic astrology. For Aquarius, understanding the Leo archetype is just as beneficial as understanding their own Aquarian nature.

If you know you have Aquarius as your South Node, you probably will gain even more benefits by reading the Leo chapter as well. Pay close attention to how you spend your leisure time. Don't neglect your hobbies. Speak your free mind more. Fight the urge to distance yourself from family and friends, even if they can be "difficult".

## Root Karmic Triggers for Aquarius

The phrase "root karmic triggers" refers to people, things, and situations that are most likely to reflect or highlight a person's karma from birth, based on their sun sign. Think of them as "sensitive" areas, if you like. These often contain deep vulnerabilities within the psyche of the Aquarius archetype, and hide an uncultivated wellspring of great, transcendent power if the appropriate conscious work is put in to transform weakness into strength.

It is highly generalized – no two Aquarians are exactly the same, after all – and should be taken with a reasonable grain of salt. However, even with the potential for some margin of error, these triggers may prove to be a common theme for many who identify under the sign of Aquarius; even those who may not have their natal sun in Aquarius (such as a Venus in Aquarius, for example). As a result, it is highly recommended that every Aquarius individual examine these areas in their life, and utilize them as opportunities to evolve:

## FALSE DETACHMENT

Aquarius can be a tough read for many. Equally comfortable staying silent or being outspoken, communicating is something they tend to do quite well, and making friends is relatively easy for the average Aquarian. The issues arise when bonds begin to form. Aquarius has often been labeled as cold and detached. This isn't always fair to them, but it stems from the sense of distance that is placed between an Aquarius and their friends or lovers. Unless they are one of the exceptions who has grown fully at home in their skin, Aquarians will generally withhold a portion of themselves back.

As relationships are built on a foundation of trust and reciprocity, this creates a ticking time bomb for the relationship.

The extremity of this varies based on the level of maturity of the Aquarius in question. On the lower levels, they are not above manipulating others or information to keep things at a certain position; but a higher-minded Aquarius will not seek to control others deliberately.

## ACCEPTING LIMITATIONS

One of the most excruciating things for an Aquarius to reconcile with is the state of things as they are now. With distant visions of future worlds that call them towards the strange and unknowns, some Aquarians struggle with adjusting to 3D reality, along with all its apparent conflicts, contradictions, and competitions. Accepting things as they are, big and small, at any given point in time, will help ground the Aquarius. Then, instead of focusing on things beyond man's control, they can direct their attention towards positive actions within their means.

## FIXED FLUIDITY

Aquarians love to flow, mingle, and mix it up with the crows. Simultaneously, they are adamant in their ways, and tend to move in a particular manner. They love to think of themselves as inclusive and understanding, even when they strongly disagree with someone's lifestyle or choices. It is at these times that the Aquarius runs the risk of compromising their truth, which may be grating or intimidating to some initially. But the world will benefit much more from an honest Aquarius that speaks their truth, instead of one that denies it.

## In Short...

The most pressing lesson for sun Aquarius – as well as individuals with prominent Aquarius birth chart placements – is to not compromise who they are, what they believe, and what they know. Whether they spent the past 20 years researching the most esoteric topics, or woke up from a dream that revealed obscure knowledge that hasn't been heard in centuries, Aquarians are natural repositories for information. As the living embodiment of the world wide web, they are tailor made to share as well as help new and innovative ideas circulate. Aquarius makes a great philanthropist, for this reason.

Aquarians can sometimes fall prey to hypocrisy, which can be avoided by practicing tolerance of differing views and opinions. It doesn't matter how beneficial becoming a vegan for you was; forcing someone who loves eating fried chicken to quit won't make anyone happy (sorry chickens). Every Aquarius should reflect often on the thing they treasure above all else: personal freedom.

Therefore, honor everyone's personal freedom as much as you honor yours (provided they are not putting anyone in harm's way). And you'd be surprised how much of that "change" you secretly long for would take shape in your environment, through your simply living in accordance with the rhythm of your internal truth.

If you identify with Aquarius, ask yourself the following questions:

1. When I listen to others, am I really hearing them?

2. What can I do to bridge the gap

between myself and others?

3. Am I willing to tell the truth, the whole truth, and nothing but the truth?

Answer these questions honestly, and reflect on each of them afterwards to ascertain where you currently are on your life journey from a karma-clearing perspective.

# 12

# PISCES: BETWEEN WORLDS

**Affirmation:** "I am everything; and, everything is me."

Of all the zodiac signs, Pisces may be the hardest to pin down and figure out. Two fishes swimming in opposite directions (or circling each other, depending on how one views it) is the perfect symbolism to express the Piscean journey.

The twelfth and final sign of the zodiac represents the sum total of all shared lessons and experiences: from Aries' need to establish themselves, all the way to Aquarius' concerns towards the greater group and society. That leaves Pisces with the unenviable task of putting it all together, and bringing it to fruition, and into the next level of awareness.

## Common Karmic Lessons

If Aries is the alpha, then Pisces is the omega. As a mutable water sign, Pisces embodies the totality of every lesson learned by the previous 11 signs. It also, of course, comes with its own particular challenges. Being a Pisces is like being continually submerged in the deepest waters without warning, without a rope, floatie, or scuba gear. Sink, or swim.

Consider the life of Edgar Cayce. He was a humble man, who for all intents and purposes was just a regular guy on the surface – until bedtime. Cayce became renowned worldwide for his ability to channel messages and relay highly occult and specific information in his trance states. The information he shared was always accurate – where it could be verified – and ran the gamut from healing foods and herbs, to the origins of man, and ancient civilizations such as Lemuria and Atlantis.

No; every Pisces is not Mr. Cayce. However, within every Pisces is the potential to sink into that primordial ocean we call mind, and swim back with artifacts and treasures the rest of the world may have forgotten ever existed. This is because Pisces are highly attuned to feminine energetic frequencies. These raise one's level of receptivity, promoting a state of near total submission. This allows them to receive the more subtle messages from "the universe", if you will. This is not an ability exclusive to Pisces; they are simply the most naturally synced to it.

So where's the challenge? As highly-sensitive and empathic people, Pisces run the risk of "dissolving" their sense of self, falling prey to escapism when "the real world" rears its ugly head, and developing extremely superstitious behaviors. It is imperative most of all for the Pisces to learn how to live in the world, though not of it.

## Karmic Clues by Nodes

Opposite to Pisces is the sixth house ruler, Virgo. In everyone's birth chart there is a North Node (also known as Rahu), and a South Node (also known as Ketu). The sign our South Node is in speaks to where we're coming from as a sentient soul –

or in other words, our recent past lives, and predominant mindsets and skillsets as a result. The sign of our North Node – which is always approximate 180 degrees apart from the South Node, just as Virgo always rests 180 degrees opposite Pisces – represents the areas of life we are less comfortable in or accustomed to, but will lead to the most growth and fulfillment for the soul, when pursued and developed.

In other words, the South Node sign can be said to reflect the things that come easy to us (our comfort zones), whereas the North Node represents the things that only come with conscious, deliberate effort (our greatest growth opportunities). Understanding the Nodes and their role in our destiny (that is, destination), is vital to understanding our karmic astrology. For Pisces, understanding the Virgo archetype is just as beneficial as understanding their own Piscean nature.

If you know you have Pisces as your South Node, you probably will gain even more benefits by reading the Virgo chapter as well. Give to others in a way that agrees with your well-being. Pay close attention to how you give and share with others. Set healthy limits, with reasonable boundaries, and avoid any tendencies to become a martyr and self-sacrifice unnecessarily.

## Root Karmic Triggers for Pisces

The phrase "root karmic triggers" refers to people, things, and situations that are most likely to reflect or highlight a person's karma from birth, based on their sun sign. Think of them as "sensitive" areas, if you like. These often contain deep vulnerabilities within the psyche of the

Pisces archetype, and hide an uncultivated wellspring of great, transcendent power if the appropriate conscious work is put in to transform weakness into strength.

It is highly generalized – no two Pisces are exactly the same, after all – and should be taken with a reasonable grain of salt. However, even with the potential for some margin of error, these triggers may prove to be a common theme for many who identify under the sign of Pisces; even those who may not have their natal sun in Pisces (such as a moon in Pisces, for example). As a result, it is highly recommended that every Pisces individual examine these areas in their life, and utilize them as opportunities to evolve:

## THE FEET

Every sign rules over certain areas of the body. Pisces rules over the feet. Every Pisces has a bit of a monk or ascetic buried within them – one who has traversed over hot coals, scorching deserts, jagged plains, and dry grasslands. Just ask a Pisces for their opinion on a random subject, and there's a good chance they'll have a solid answer that sounds reasonable, even if they have next-to-no firsthand experience with the subject. Don't let their age fool you: those feet have seen more than their share of concrete.

Metaphorically, Pisces often act as the "feet" of their social circles. With friends and family alike, its not uncommon for a Pisces to bear the burdens of others on top of their own. In one sense, the Pisces should actively work to fight the urge to place undue weight on their own backs.

In another sense, Pisces should take good care of their feet, as they are a greatly overlooked source of receiving information. Go for barefoot walks in the earth. Treat them to the occasional foot bath. Keep those lower veins circulating!

## THE FALSE

As a natural receptor to spiritual insights and intuition, one of the greatest dangers facing a Pisces is the allure of illusions, and deceptive thoughts. For a Pisces, the non-real isn't hard to confuse with what is. This becomes an even greater predicament where the consumption of intoxicants is indulged. Pisces rules the twelfth house of the subconscious, and they reflect these same traits. In other words: the mind of Pisces is a non-discriminative breeding ground for all things of the imagination;

and that can go either way. Unfortunately, too many of the past chose paranoia over peace.

Since Pisces is the furthest sign from Aries on the astrological wheel, by this point, the self-identity that was so hard fought for in previous incarnations may now act as a distant memory. Some Pisces find it easier to lean into their empathic sensitivities. Seeking to blend with others, and not caring to bring their own sense of self along with, wires can get easily crossed, and something more valuable than the Pisces realized may be lost in the process.

## THE FAITH

Religion is voluntary, but spirituality is mandatory. This is self-evident once one recognizes what it means to be spiritual... and this understanding comes naturally to most Pisces, who already walk between two worlds. In the known, visiting from the unknown.

Imagine what it might feel like to come to Earth as an extra-terrestrial. Your mammoth mothership lands, your team engages in scouting and excavation excursions, your group is spotted by the locals, a panic ensues, and in all the ruckus, you've become stranded as you watch your mothership take off into the deep night without you. Not a fun feeling, is it? Well, that's how a lot of Pisces feel on planet Earth, right now.

The world can be a cold, dark, confusing place. Sometimes it appears more chaotic than orderly, and it can be difficult distinguishing people's true intentions. The answer to fears, doubts, and every single internal conflict, is to go within, and connect to that ever-knowing center. We all have it; we all can consult it. And Pisces have all-access – should they choose to make use of it. All it requires is a measure of faith no larger than a grain of teff.

## In Short...

The most pressing lesson for sun Pisces – as well as individuals with prominent Pisces birth chart placements – is learning how to fully love the world and all it contains... including themselves, as they are. There's nothing wrong with the occasional daydream or playful dance through half-sleep reverie. However, too much time spent in the intangible world, will more than likely have a negative impact on the Pisces once they return to the material world.

Reconciling the spiritual and the physical, is the great and noble task assigned to all Pisces willing to accept the challenge. As they are more inclined towards the intangible, exercises and activities that help center their consciousness in the tangible will put both aspects of their world on the same page. Drugs, cults, and anything that caters to the Piscean tendency to veer towards excess ought to be avoided at all costs. (This extends to relationships rooted in toxic dynamics.)

This is a call to action to all Pisces: accept yourself. Accept the world. See you in the world, and the world in you. Integrate the two. And, once you have succeeded in seeing the One: share your findings with the rest of the class.

If you identify with Pisces, ask yourself the following questions:

1. Why am I drawn to what I'm drawn to?

2. Am I making enough time for nothing regularly?

3. Did that person I wanted to help ask to be helped?

Answer each question honestly, and reflect on them afterwards to determine how you are currently progressing on your karmic journey.

# AFTERWORD

The following websites will allow you to construct your own birth chart. They are simple to use, and are free as well (at the time of this publication):

1. www.astro.com/horoscope (my go-to for years)

2. horoscopes.astro-seek.com/birth-chart-horoscope-online (no account needed)

3. astro.cafeastrology.com (haven't

used personally; but an option)

There are other sites beyond these three as well. As it pertains to identifying your likeliest root karmic triggers: study closely the position and planetary aspects made to/by your following placements...

rising (1st house),

4th house,

7th house (especially concerning your relationships and partnerships)

midheaven (10th house),

south node (what your soul has most mastered),

and north node (what your soul most yearns to experience).

Above all else: I wish you the very best health, wealth, and success, all throughout your karmic journey across the stars.

# ABOUT THE AUTHOR

As a wearer of many hats, and a seeker of many passions, **Copper Moon's** indigenous American background included an early introduction into the universality of man's eternal soul, and the innate oneness of all life. During adolescence, Moon was "accidentally" introduced early on to astrology, by way of scouring family bookshelves.

Titles such as Linda Goodman's Sun Signs, and The Hidden Power of Everyday Things had had a profound impact that expanded the possibilities of life's potential meanings, as well as how life & truth could express itself. This eventually led to the study of related fields that included numerology and palmistry.

Before graduating high school, Moon had learned how to draw and analyze birth charts by hand, and had performed this service for several family members, friends, and acquaintances. Money was never a part of this equation. It was strictly the love of learning more about the human condition, and delighting others with glimpses into themselves that even they had overlooked, that motivated this impromptu hobby organically.

Not long after enrolling in university, Moon abandoned the world of astrology for many years, for reasons related to unreconciled religious conflicts. These mental conflicts were later resolved upon further meditations and reflections, and the practice of reading birth charts was resumed by request. Rather than considering themselves as a professional astrologer, as there is almost an impossible number of components to study in the subject within a single lifetime, the author simply prefers to think of themselves as "a lifelong student of the stars."

**All About Astrology and Tarot**
Word Search

**The Hidden Secret of God:**
The Bible Decoded
by Neville Goddard

**Spirit Speaks
Louder Than Words:**
An Unconventional Memoir

**Meditation in 7 Pages**


**Finding Your Voice:**
A Practical Self Help Guide
to Stop Stuttering


**The Little Blue Book:**
(aka El Librito Azul)
Metaphysics in Simple Terms

www.ingramcontent.com/pod-product-compliance
Lightning Source LLC
Chambersburg PA
CBHW011222120626
46545CB00010B/3105